THE HAYWOODS, COLWICH, MILFORD and BROCTON

A Portrait in Old Picture Postcards

by
Roy Lewis

GW00569863

S. B. Publications

**This book is dedicated to my wife, my sons, and their families,
who have all enjoyed exploring the Chase and its neighbourhood.**

First published in 1993 by S.B. Publications,
c/o 19 Grove Road, Seaford, East Sussex BN25 1TP

ISBN 1 85770.051.1

Typeset, printed and bound by Manchester Free Press,
Longford Trading Estate, Thomas Street, Stretford Manchester M32 0JT.

CONTENTS

Page

Introduction .... v-vi
GREAT HAYWOOD — The Square 1-3
The Clifford Arms 4-5
Trent Lane 6
The station 7
Essex Bridge 8-9
Canal lock, Trent Lane 10
Mill and canal wharf 11
Motor accident at the mill 12-13
High Street 14
Fanny Crook's shop 15
Main Road 16
St John's R.C. Church 17
Main Road 18
Fox Cottages 19
Village scene 20
St Stephen's church 21
The Memorial Hall 22
LITTLE HAYWOOD — The Red Lion 23
Main Road 24

Page

LITTLE HAYWOOD — Meadow Lane 25
G.H. Smith's shop 26
Meadow Lane 27
Wooden Bridge 28
Weetman's Bridge 29
The Lamb and Flag 30
Main Road 31-32
Station Road 33
COLWICH — St Benedict's Priory 34-35
The Station 36
The church and vicarage 37
Village scene 38
Canal lock 39
BISHTON — Bishton Lane 40
Bishton Hall 41
WOLSELEY BRIDGE — The Roebuck 42
Cromwell House 43
Wolseley Hall 44
Stafford Road 45
CANNOCK CHASE — Satnall Hills 46

CONTENTS

Page

SHUGBOROUGH — The Hall 47
The Stafford Lodge 48
The Essex Bridge Lodge 49
The Triumphal Arch 50
The Tunnel, West Portal 51
Railway Bridge 52
TIXALL — St John The Baptist Church 53
Hall and Gatehouse 54
Bottle Lodge 55
Staffordshire Yeomanry 56-57
INGESTRE — Hall 58
Royal visit to the Hall 59
Church 60-61
MILFORD — Station 62
Station Road on Milford Day 63
Easter 64
Donkeys on the Chase 65
The Barley Mow 66
Club outing 67
The Common 68

Page

MILFORD — The Rock House 69
Stafford Road 70-71
Sister Dora Convalescent Hosp 72
The Chase 73
The Golf House 74-75
BROCTON — The Hall 76
Pool Lane 77
The Green 78-79
Oldacre Lane 80
The Chase 81
BROCTON CAMP — Roadworks 82
Military Police 83
L and M Lines 84
Church parade 85
Home Hut, J Lines 86
Officer's Club 87
Greetings card 88
Sketch map of the district 89
S.B. Publications 90
Front Cover: Shugborough Hall, Great Haywood

INTRODUCTION

This book covers the old parishes of Colwich (including Great and Little Haywood), Tixall, Ingestre, and those parts of Baswich not illustrated in *Stafford and District : A Portrait in Old Picture Postcards*. The geography of the area is determined by the River Trent and its tributary, the Sow, which joins the Trent at Great Haywood. Along the line of these rivers were constructed the main roads, and later the canals and railways. The main road from London to the whole of north-west England crossed the area by way of Wolseley Bridge (where a branch diverted through Milford to Stafford), Colwich, Little and Great Haywood. It is only in recent years that a by-pass has carried traffic away from these villages

The postcards chosen for this book date from 1903 to 1939. At that time this was a rural area with a total population of not much more than 2,000 people, most of whom were tradesmen or connected with farming. It was an area of large estates and families who had held their land for centuries; although the conversion of the great houses to other uses had begun before 1939.

By 1903 Milford Common or Chase, and the adjacent parts of Cannock Chase, had become a tourist attraction drawing crowds of railway passengers, walkers and cyclists, especially on summer weekends and bank holidays. The influx of visitors provided additional employment in the tea-rooms and apartments which catered for the visitors. The number of visitors encouraged postcard publishers to provide a plentiful variety of cards for sale in shops and tea-rooms throughout the district.

In compiling this book I have tried to select those cards which provide the best record of the district before 1939, and also to include, as far as possible cards which have not been reproduced before. All the cards are from my own collection.

The cards are arranged as a tour of the area. Starting at The Square, Great Haywood, we go first north and then south along the main street of Great Haywood. The tour continues thorough Little Haywood, Colwich, and Bishton to Wolseley Bridge. It then doubles back across the Chase to Shugborough and Milford before making detours, first to Tixall and Ingestre, and then to Brocton. The book ends with a small selection of cards relating to the World War I army camp at Brocton.

Postcards are notoriously difficult to date since publication is sometimes years after the photograph on which the card is based. Dates given in the book are best guesses arrived at by a mixture of internal evidence, postmark date where a card has been postally used, and a study of postcard publishers.

In putting this book together I have been helped by many people who have recalled the scenes on the postcards, by librarians who have found books and information, and by historians who have made available the results of their own inquiries. To all of them, too numerous to list by name, I record my grateful thanks. They have made the writing of this book a journey of discovery and pleasure. I hope those who read the book will share this with me.

Those who wish to know more about the area should read:

Stafforda — *Guide and History of Ancient Haywood* (1924) and Supplement

C.J. and J.P. Whitehouse — *A Town for Four Winters* (1983)

K. Judkins — *My Life in Steam* (1970) — early chapters relate to this area

Great Haywood through the eyes of its children — a delightful book of children's work produced by Anson C.E. (A) school in 1991.

Roy Lewis
The Oak House
Crescent Road
Stafford.

Great Haywood

THE SQUARE, GREAT HAYWOOD, 1905

The Square is the heart of Great Haywood. Until recent years the main highway from London to the whole of north-west England passed this way and was joined in the Square by Trent Lane, the way to Shugborough. Note the National Cyclists Union badge on the corner of the Clifford Arms.

THE SQUARE, GREAT HAYWOOD, 1907

This postcard shows the Square looking north from the entrance to Trent Lane. The two trees in the foreground were planted in the nineteenth century to commemorate Queen Victoria's Jubilee. One foggy night in the late 1920s, when there were road works in The Square, a lorry driver, confused by the lamps marking the road works, drove into one tree and snapped it off. A few years later the other died. Across the Square, next to S. Adkin's butcher's shop, can be seen the post office. Later this became a cobbler's shop, popular with children because the cobbler would always put a hobnail in the point of their top to make it spin more readily.

The Village — Great Haywood

THE SQUARE, GREAT HAYWOOD, 1903

The third view shows the west side of the Square with the Clifford Arms Hotel on the left. This was once the gatehouse to Haywood Hall, the home of the Astons before they moved to Tixall Hall in the sixteenth century. The front of the Hotel was rebuilt in the nineteenth century. Barbara Aston, the last of the Aston family, married the Hon. Thomas Clifford, and the Hotel takes its name from this family. The waggon passing the Clifford Arms belonged to William Tooth, a local man, who ran a carrier's service for people and parcels into Stafford every Saturday.

Clifford Arms, Great Haywood. South View.

THE CLIFFORD ARMS, 1908

This postcard of the back of The Clifford Arms shows how much older the building was than its nineteenth-century facade. Parts had remained unchanged since the sixteenth century, and may have been part of the original gatehouse. Carriages and coaches could drive under the central arch into the yard where an ostler was employed to look after the horses. Notice the water pump and horse trough on the right.

Clifford Arms Hotel, Great Haywood.

THE CLIFFORD ARMS, 1927

In the 1920s the street front of the Clifford Arms was given a face-lift with a mock black and white facade thought to be more in keeping with the age of the building. In 1930, after a change of ownership, it was decided to pull the old building down and build a new modern hotel on the site. That is the building you can see today.

TRENT LANE, GREAT HAYWOOD, 1939

Trent Lane was the way to Shugborough. In 1806 the houses seen here were built to give the approach a fitting appearance and provide homes for staff. Among those who have lived here was James Vickerstaff, a gardener, whose step-daughter seduced a young doctor's assistant at Haywood, and eloped with him and her step-father's savings. William Palmer, the assistant, was rescued by his family and grew up to be the notorious Rugeley poisoner. The railway bridge, added in 1848, was designed to be in keeping with the other buildings. The post office was moved to the house on the right in 1908. In 1939 it was kept by Mrs Yelland.

GREAT HAYWOOD STATION, 1918

Walk down Trent Lane and look for a grassy path sloping upwards near the railway bridge. This was once the way to Great Haywood station. When the Trent Valley line was built in 1848 it had to cross the Shugborough estate. Lord Lichfield gave permission only on condition that a station was built at Haywood and that, at his request, any train on the line would stop there for his family and guests to board or alight. The station was closed in the 1960s.

ESSEX BRIDGE, 1918

The story that the Earl of Essex built the bridge to allow Queen Elizabeth to visit him at Chartley Castle without having to ford the river is a romantic fiction. There has indeed been a bridge here since the sixteenth century, but it was known as Shugborough Bridge because it was the way to the village of Shugborough, which was destroyed by the Ansons as it spoiled the view from their mansion. This drawing is by H. Overton Jones, the son of a Burslem china manufacturer, who bought the Ivy House at Colwich in 1912, when he was retiring from active management of the family business.

Copyright
G.H.6.

The River, Great Haywood.

ESSEX BRIDGE, 1933

Essex Bridge has always been for horses and foot travellers. The parapets are low to avoid pack horses' bulky loads rubbing on the stonework and the angular bays, clearly seen above, allowed people to stand aside when a horse was crossing. Alongside the bridge was a shallow ford which allowed carts and carriages to cross. Today this provides a shallow children's paddling place.

CANAL LOCK, TRENT LANE, GREAT HAYWOOD, 1932

The Trent and Mersey Canal, following the line of the Trent valley, was opened as far as this lock on 24 June 1770. By the following September it was extended to Weston. The lock-keeper's house is on the right, with a warehouse and basin for unloading boats beyond it. The basin is now filled in. As the use of the canal declined the lock-keeper opened a tea-room for visitors in part of the building. The sign TEAS on the warehouse can be seen clearly in this view.

THE MILL AND CANAL WHARF, GREAT HAYWOOD, 1907

This was once the busiest junction on the whole of the canal system. The bridge in the centre carried the towpath of the Trent and Mersey canal over the Staffordshire and Worcestershire canal, which commenced here. The buildings nearby are those of the wharf with warehouses, stabling and the wharfinger's house with its two-storied octagonal bay window. In 1972 the wharf became the touring and hire base for Anglo-Welsh narrowboats. The building on the far left is a corn mill powered by water from the River Trent, which is carried under the canal near the mill.

GREAT HAYWOOD MILL.

MOTOR ACCIDENT AT GREAT HAYWOOD MILL, 1905 (**1**)

In 1905 the road from Tixall to Great Haywood made a sharp S bend to cross the Trent just north of Haywood Mill. On 9 March 1905 Mrs Challenor, wife of the Town Clerk of Hanley, and her niece were being driven across this bridge when the car's steering failed. The car plunged through the parapet and somersaulted into the river. The chauffeur jumped clear and managed to pull Mrs Challenor out of the water. This postcard shows the scene after the car was recovered from the river, with sightseers looking over the boarded-up parapet. The road was straightened and a new bridge built in 1936.

MOTOR ACCIDENT AT GREAT HAYWOOD, 1905 (2)

The body of Mrs Challenor's niece could not be found after the accident. It was thought to be trapped at the spot shown in this postcard where the outfall from the mill had scoured a 20-foot-deep hole in the river bed. The pool was dragged and divers brought in from the Manchester Ship Canal, but without success. Finally it was decided to divert the river. This postcard shows the fire engines assembled to pump the pool dry while the river was diverted. The brother of the missing woman can be seen wading in the pool with a hooked pole.

The body was eventually recovered, three weeks later, half a mile downstream.

HIGH STREET, GREAT HAYWOOD.

HIGH STREET, GREAT HAYWOOD, 1907

This view of the Main Road, looking north, is still recognisable today. Most of the houses remain, although April Cottage, on the far left, no longer has a bay window. The three children lived in the cottage or one of the nearby houses. The older girl, carrying a can, was on her way to fetch milk when stopped by the photographer. Note the boy's typical Eton collar, Norfolk jacket and boots.

FANNY CROOK'S SHOP, GREAT HAYWOOD, 1907

Fanny opened her shop in 1907 and sold everything from Beecham's pills to furniture polish, including postcards, some of which can be seen in the shop window. If you look at the view of the High Street on the opposite page, Fanny's shop, with its outside steps and iron handrail, is on the far right by the telegraph pole. Fanny had this postcard printed, showing her on the doorstep of her new shop, to send to friends asking for their custom.

15

Copyright
G.H. 3.

The Village, Great Haywood.

MAIN ROAD, GREAT HAYWOOD, 1933

This view looks south from the corner of Brewery Lane towards the Clifford Arms. The tall house on the
left still stands on the corner of Brewery Lane. In 1933 it was the home of W. Buttery, undertaker, whose
place of work lay behind the house. On the right are Trent Villa and Holmleigh, built by Joe Bradbury,
farmer and blacksmith, about 1906. Holmleigh was the home of Mary Hill, the village schoolmistress, and
later of her nephew, Philip Thornton. He was an internationally-known engraver and clockmaker. His sign
can be seen in the picture, just above the tall hedge on the right.

239-5. St. John's Church, Great Haywood.

ST JOHN'S R.C. CHURCH, GREAT HAYWOOD, 1927

This church was originally built in 1829 as a family chapel for the Clifford family at Tixall Hall. When the family left Tixall in 1845 the church was carefully taken down stone by stone and rebuilt on its present site at Great Haywood. At the same time a school was built on an adjoining site. When the present Roman Catholic primary school was built in 1962 the old school was closed and pulled down.

MAIN ROAD, GREAT HAYWOOD, 1927

This postcard shows the High Street looking south from the corner of Tixall Road. When this card was printed, James Morrough, painter and decorator, had just opened a newsagent's shop, which can be seen on the left. Today the building is still recognisable, although the small bay windows have been replaced by the larger windows of the Spar. The house on the far left is now a butcher's shop. All the cottages on the right have been pulled down to allow road improvement. Their site is now part of the grass verge outside Haywood Abbey Nursing Home.

The Fox Cottages, Great Haywood.

FOX COTTAGES, GREAT HAYWOOD, 1927

'The Fox and Hounds' was here as long ago as 1834, when William Dawson was the landlord and kept a shop as well. The nearby cottages were known as Fox Cottages. Note the water butts to collect rainwater from the roofs in the days before the cottages had a mains water supply. Today the cottage on the far right is pulled down and the others incorporated in the public house. A little way past these cottages was the tollgate where travellers once stopped to pay toll before travelling on this road. The gatekeeper had a son who, even at the age of seven, attracted the attention of travellers as he sat drawing by the gate. He grew up to be the artist, Thomas Peploe Wood.

Great Haywood. Staffs.

GREAT HAYWOOD, 1907

This is the view you would have had if you had stood in The Square and looked towards Little Haywood in 1907. On the far left the sign 'Post Office' can be seen on the wall. Next door is the shop of J. Leaver, saddler and harness maker, with its stable-like half door. On the right is the blacksmith's house with his smithy lying back from the road. Today, except for the old Post Office and a much-altered cottage on the far right, every house shown on this postcard has been pulled down.

ST STEPHEN'S CHURCH, GREAT HAYWOOD, 1905

Great Haywood was, for many years, divided between the parishes of Colwich and Stowe-by-Chartley, and had no parish church of its own. In the 1840s Lord Lichfield built a chapel of ease here for the villagers, and in 1854 Great Haywood became a separate parish with St Stephen's as its parish church. The original design was by Thomas Trubshaw, the local architect and builder. It was altered even before it was built, and there have been later additions and alterations.

THE MEMORIAL HALL, GREAT HAYWOOD, 1927

This memorial to the men from Great Haywood who served in the first World War was built with money raised by public subscription. The foundation stone was laid by 9-year-old Viscount Anson in July 1922, and the hall opened in the following December. It is said to have been the first building in Great Haywood to have had a piped water supply: Lord Lichfield having laid a pipe from Shugborough Hall over the River Trent. Note the dates 1914 — 1919 (the date of the Peace Treaty) instead of the usual 1918 (the date of the Armistice).

THE RED LION, LITTLE HAYWOOD, 1908

This old public house was once The Bowyer Arms, named after the family who at that time owned Bishton Hall. Its sign was the arms of the Bowyers, which included a rampant red lion. In time the public house changed its name to The Red Lion. The first known licensees in the eighteenth century were John Dean, who had been in service as a footman at Hoar Cross Hall, and his wife, who had risen from being a maid at Tixall Hall to being lady's maid to the Duchess of Norfolk. In 1908 the licensee was William Labram. The public house was rebuilt in the 1930s.

LITTLE HAYWOOD, 1910

The photographer who took this picture was standing at the crossroads in Little Haywood, with Coley Lane on his right, and Meadow Lane behind the man with his hands in his pockets. The Red Lion can be seen in the distance. Most of the houses are still standing, but the one on the left has been pulled down.

MEADOW LANE, LITTLE HAYWOOD, 1910

The photographer who took the photograph on the opposite page turned his camera to look down Meadow Lane. Today the three storied house on the right is long gone, and the house next to it is much altered. The cart in the distance stands outside the butcher's shop of G.H. Smith. The man in the milk float in the foreground, with a churn full of milk waiting to be delivered to houses in the village, is probably Christopher Sproston, whose family had a farm further down Meadow Lane.

G. H. SMITH'S SHOP, MEADOW LANE, LITTLE HAYWOOD, 1907

The Smith family owned a farm where 'The Stables' development is today. About 1906 they opened this shop in Meadow Lane. The postcard shows George Smith himself in the centre, with his assistant and a boy. It was usual at that time to hang meat outside a shop, although a special display would have been put on for the photograph. Notice the pig's head and the straw spread to keep down the dust. This card was sent to the wife of the Vicar of Ingestre with the message, 'With thanks for past orders and the hope to receive a further share of your patronage.'

MEADOW LANE, LITTLE HAYWOOD, 1910
The road bridge over the Trent and Mersey Canal, and the bridge by which the railway crossed Meadow Lane, can be seen clearly in the distance. Between the two bridges is Navigation Farm, which was at one time an inn.

Old Wooden Bridge — Meadow Lane — Little Haywood

WOODEN BRIDGE, MEADOW LANE, LITTLE HAYWOOD

Before 1830 everyone who went along Meadow Lane had to cross the Trent by a shallow ford. One writer described seeing, 'On bright sunny days, mothers with their tiny ones (shoes and stockings in hand) merrily wading through the stream'. In winter the crossing was less pleasant. In 1830 a bridge was erected so that those on foot could cross with dry feet. Cattle and carriages continued to use the ford. This postcard is postmarked 1904, but the picture is much older, probably dating from the 1880s.

WEETMAN'S BRIDGE, LITTLE HAYWOOD, 1908

The wooden bridge on the opposite page was in urgent need of repair by the 1880s. In 1887 a public subscription was launched to raise money for a new bridge which would commemorate Queen Victoria's Golden Jubilee. The architect was Robert Griffiths of Stafford, and the largest subscriber Mr Weetman.

After it was built, what should have been the Jubilee Bridge came to be called Weetman's Bridge.

THE LAMB AND FLAG, LITTLE HAYWOOD, 1907

The Lamb and Flag is an old public house. The Lamb of God carrying a banner with a red cross, originally the badge of the Templars, was a popular inn sign. In the early 1920s the public house was described as having 'a spacious yard to hold conveyances which come in summer laden with people who, after roaming about the Chase, are always ready for tea with ham and eggs.' The post office to the right of The Lamb and Flag had a bakehouse round the corner in Meadow Lane. The delivery van in this picture is loading bread and cake before setting out on its round.

MAIN ROAD, LITTLE HAYWOOD, 1939

By the 1930s the post office had moved, from being next to The Lamb and Flag, to the shop on the left in this postcard view. Notice the early public telephone kiosk next to the post office. Further along the road can be seen the house where the District Bank opened for business one day a week. A manager came out from Stafford with his gladstone bag, and all the shopkeepers and tradesmen walked across to pay in their week's takings.

MAIN ROAD, LITTLE HAYWOOD, 1907

A much earlier view of the Main Road taken from nearer Colwich than the view on page 31. The ivy-clad houses still stand, although stripped of their ivy. Beyond them, through the trees, can be seen 'High Chase', then the home of Norwood Young and later of Robert Copeland, a member of the well-known family of china manufacturers. Today High Chase Road has been built over the grounds of Norwood Young's house, although two of the trees shown in this picture still survive.

STATION ROAD, LITTLE HAYWOOD.

STATION ROAD, LITTLE HAYWOOD, 1907

If the photographer who took the picture on the opposite page had turned and pointed his camera towards Colwich, this is the picture he would have taken. In fact the shadows show that the two views were not taken at the same time. On the left, beyond the ivy-clad houses, is the angled row of three cottages known as Tub Row. These were pulled down when St Mary's Road was built. On the other side of the road, beyond the house where the Trubshaws used to live, much of the wall was pulled down when Hawkesmore Drive was laid out.

St. Benedict's Priory, Colwich. Entrance.

ST BENEDICT'S PRIORY, COLWICH, 1922

Charles Trubshaw built a house on this site about 1730 and called it Mount Pleasant. A century later it was sold to Lord Tamworth who enlarged it and renamed it Mount Pavilion. Unfortunately he died before the house was ready for occupation and it was resold. The new owners were a group of French Benedictine nuns who, after escaping the guillotine in revolutionary France, had had several homes in England before buying Mount Pavilion. Over the years they have added to the house. This view shows the older gothic building and the later, contrasting wing on the right.

St. Benedict's Priory, Colwich. Refectory.

REFECTORY, ST BENEDICT'S PRIORY, COLWICH, 1922

In 1922 the nuns commissioned a set of nine (or more) postcards of the Priory from the London firm of Marshall, Keene, & Co. These give a good picture of the interior and exterior of the Priory at that time. The cards above and on the opposite page are both from this set. Note the plain wooden stools, simple furnishings, and the desk from which a suitable text would be read during otherwise silent meals. Today the Community has been renamed St Mary's Abbey.

COLWICH STATION, 1904

The Trent Valley line to London was opened in 1847, and that is the date of Colwich station and the station-master's house, seen on the left. Colwich was also the place where the London North Western Railway and the 'Notty', or North Staffordshire Railway, met, so that the station was jointly managed. Ken Judkins, in his autobiography, wrote of Colwich, 'My dad was a 'Railway Servant' on the London North Western. The black shiny locomotives impresses me as a boy and I was sometimes taken on the footplate. The 'Notty' made the initial running-in trip of all new engines to our station.'

COLWICH CHURCH AND VICARAGE, 1914

There was a medieval church here, but little remains of it. The tower is dated 1640 and much of the rest was rebuilt in Victorian times. Inside are memorials to Admiral Anson, who circumnavigated the world, and Field Marshal Lord Wolseley, a distinguished soldier and the model for the 'Modern Major General' in Gilbert and Sullivan's *Pirates of Penzance*. The east window, seen here, is a memorial to the first Earl of Lichfield. The large Victorian vicarage was, in 1914, the home of Prebendary Dobree, well known for the tricycle on which he rode everywhere, and for continuing as vicar until he was well over 90 years of age.

COLWICH, 1904

This is part of the main road from London to Manchester, Liverpool and the north west. The postcard shows how little traffic there was even on a main road in 1904. Nellie came to Colwich on holiday in July 1905, and this is the postcard she bought in the village and sent home to Seacombe. She stayed with her cousins in the School House and marked it with a cross.

CANAL LOCK, COLWICH, 1908

A view of the Trent and Mersey Canal with the lock-keeper's house in the centre. In 1839 this was the scene of a notorious murder. Mrs Christina Collins, a passenger on a narrow-boat bound for London, was attacked by two drunken boatmen after passing through this lock. She attempted to escape and 'got her legs half way into the water' before being hauled back, raped and murdered. Her body was dumped in the canal at Rugeley. Her attackers were hanged and Mrs Collins buried in the churchyard at Rugeley. 'The Wench is Dead', one of Colin Dexter's Chief Inspector Morse novels, was inspired by this murder.

BISHTON LANE, 1908

The hamlet of Bishton lies 200 yards off the main Colwich to Wolseley Bridge road. The Bishop of Chester once owned the manor, and its name is a corruption of Bishop's tun (or hamlet). The houses in this view were built in the nineteenth century to house the bailiff and estate workers from Bishton Hall.

BISHTON HALL, 1939

The de Bishton family, and later the Bowyers and the Sneyds, had a house on this site. In the late-eighteenth century it was bought by a banker, John Sparrow, who pulled down the old house and built the one shown here. He also laid out the grounds and built a Greek temple in them. After he died his unmarried daughter, Charlotte, lived here and added the two bow fronted blocks on either side of the entrance. She was responsible for the first school in Colwich and her death is still remembered each year by the pupils. The Hall is now the home of St. Bede's School.

THE ROEBUCK, WOLSELEY BRIDGE, 1908

This inn was originally The Wolseley Arms, changed its name to The Roebuck, and has now reverted to its original name. The junction of two main roads here made the inn an important meeting place in the eighteenth century. Mail coaches stopped here to change horses and pick up mail. In 1908 the inn was kept by Ralph Gee, better known as 'Owd Raff'. Gee was also a contractor who operated several steam-driven lorries for haulage and owned a number of threshing machines which went round neighbouring farms.

CROMWELL HOUSE, WOLSELEY BRIDGE, 1935

Early in the Civil War a body of Parliamentary soldiers guarding the river crossing at Wolseley Bridge was surprised and routed by Royalist troops under Major Scudamore, just before the Battle of Hopton Heath (1643). In the 1920s the building shown on this postcard was part of Roebuck Farm. In the 1930s the farmer's wife opened a cafe and tea-rooms to cater for visitors to the Chase. She called it Cromwell House, although Cromwell had not been in charge of the Parliamentary troops here in 1643. Today it is Oliver's Restaurant.

WOLSELEY HALL, 1910

The Wolseley family have been here since Norman times and Sir Charles Wolseley still owns 1,000 acres in the area. The Old Hall was abandoned in the eighteenth century and the new Hall, seen in this postcard, built soon afterwards. At the same time the grounds were laid out with shrubberies and plantations. The Hall burned down in the 1950s and the gardens were overgrown until 1990 when they were newly laid out as Wolseley Garden Park.

STAFFORD ROAD, WOLSELEY BRIDGE, 1910

This postcard shows the road from Stafford as it approaches Wolseley Bridge, with The Roebuck and Cromwell House in the distance. On the right the fenced wood rises steeply, as it still does, but on the left the trees have gone, as the road has been twice widened.

View from Milford Chase.

SATNALL HILLS, CANNOCK CHASE, 1910

Leave Wolseley Bridge and head for Milford. On the left you will find a popular parking place in a dip known as The Punch Bowl. This postcard shows the view from the slope above the Punch Bowl, looking towards the Satnall Hills and old gravel workings. Today the spoil heaps are hidden among trees. The postcard clearly shows how the landscape of the Chase has changed since 1910.

SHUGBOROUGH HALL, 1912

The Anson's original 1693 house is surrounded by later additions. The wings and their pavilions at either
end were added in the eighteenth century, and the large projecting bay seen in this view, together with the
portico at the front entrance seen in the cover picture, about 1800. The terraced lawns with clipped yews
were laid out in the 1850s on the site of the old bowling green. The dog in the foreground is buried in the
pets' cemetery under the trees in front of the old stable block.

SHUGBOROUGH, THE STAFFORD LODGE, 1907

When Samuel Wyatt laid out Shugborough Park for Thomas Anson in the early 1800s, he designed new lodges for each drive. Each lodge was a pair of stone cubes with pyramid roofs, and pillars and niches at the front. The wrought iron gate posts and the lodge buildings were ornamented with crowns, the Anson crest. This lodge stands at the Milford entrance to Shugborough.

SHUGBOROUGH LODGE, GREAT HAYWOOD.

SHUGBOROUGH, THE ESSEX BRIDGE LODGE, 1907

An identical lodge to that at Milford (see the opposite page) was built at the end of Trent Lane in Great Haywood. When the railway bridge was built across the Lane, the lodge was taken down and rebuilt as the Lichfield Lodge on the Stafford to Rugeley Road. In its place was built the lodge seen above. Notice the Anson crowns on all four gateposts. In the distance can bee seen Essex Bridge.

SHUGBOROUGH, THE TRIUMPHAL ARCH, 1928

Thomas Anson, the brother of Admiral Anson, transformed the house and park at Shugborough into a splendid estate in the mid-eighteenth century. In the park he built a number of decorative buildings and monuments to improve and add interest to views. This copy of the Arch of Hadrian was one of the monuments. While it was being built, Admiral Anson died and the Arch was turned into a monument to him and his wife. Their busts were placed in the upper stages. It can still be seen between the Milford Drive and the main Stafford Road.

SHUGBOROUGH TUNNEL, WEST PORTAL, 1910

When the Trent Valley railway line was built in the 1840s, Lord Lichfield only allowed it to pass through his estate on condition the line was screened by trees and a tunnel built 'to hide the sight of trains as they pass in and out'. The tunnel is 777 yards long and had to be excavated with gunpowder, which led to a fatal accident during its construction. The west portal is deliberately modelled on the gateway to a Norman castle, with a tower on either side of the line. The other end looks like an Egyptian temple.

SHUGBOROUGH RAILWAY BRIDGE, 1924

In Shugborough park the Trent Valley railway line crossed the Lichfield Drive by this bridge. It was designed in the classical style so that it would be in keeping with park monuments like the Triumphal Arch. The plinths on top carry figures of seahorses and lions, the supporters of the Anson, or Earl of Lichfield's, coat of arms. Today it is not easy to see the bridge, even from the express trains that speed across it.

Tixall Church, STAFFORD.

ST JOHN THE BAPTIST CHURCH, TIXALL, 1910

Tixall was dominated for many years by the Aston family from Tixall Hall. The Astons, and most of those who worked for them, were Catholic. The result was that the parish church had only a tiny congregation. In 1829 it had no Sunday School, 'the children being all Catholics'. The church became so dilapidated that it was partly taken down and reduced in size. By the 1840s it was again in a dangerous state with large cracks in the walls. It was rebuilt in 1849 and has remained largely unchanged since then.

TIXALL HALL AND GATEHOUSE, 1903

The Aston family from Haywood built a house here in the sixteenth century. In 1580 Sir Walter Aston added the Gatehouse, seen here on the left. Six years later Mary Queen of Scots was imprisoned here for a fortnight while her rooms at Chartley were searched for evidence of treason. The Hall, on the right, was rebuilt in 1780. Each of the four columns of the portico at the main entrance was a single fifteen-foot-high block of local stone. The Gatehouse still stands, but the Hall was demolished in 1927 and some of the stone reused in St John's Church, Stafford. A pile of unused stone was still behind the church in 1992.

THE BOTTLE LODGE,
TIXALL, 1910

The drive from Tixall Hall crossed the Stafford to Great Haywood road and then ran across fields to near Haywood Mill. The Bottle Lodge was built at the place where the drive crossed the road. In this view, taken from the Stafford side, the drive is to the right of the Lodge. The date of the tiny, eight-sided building is uncertain, but it was probably built about 1800. It was occupied until 1927, the last inhabitant being Mrs Statham.

BOTTLE LODGE
- TIXALL -
230

STAFFORDSHIRE YEOMANRY AT TIXALL HALL, 1915

This postcard and the one on the opposite page show the Staffordshire Yeomanry in training in 1915. The unit had been mobilised in August 1914 and was quickly expanded and divided into two. The second unit, under Lt Col Sir Lovelace Stamer of Hartshill, Stoke-on-Trent, was based at Tixall Hall from its formation until October 1915. Here the guard outside the main entrance is being changed.

RECRUITING PARTY, TIXALL, 1915

The Yeomanry at Tixall was a cavalry unit. This postcard shows a recruiting party setting out from Tixall in 1915. The building behind them is the grand semi-circular stable block to the Hall, built early in the nineteenth century. One of its three 'pavilions' can be seen on the left.

South Side, Ingestre Hall.

INGESTRE HALL

The Hall, built in 1613 by Sir Walter Chetwynd on the site of an earlier house, has been described as 'the foremost display of Jacobean grandeur in the county'. In the eighteenth century it descended from the Chetwynds to the Talbots, Earls of Shrewsbury. They partly rebuilt the north and west fronts in 1809, and carefully restored the whole building after a fire in 1882. It is at present used by Sandwell Council as a residential arts centre.

ROYAL VISIT TO
INGESTRE HALL, 1907

On Monday 18 November 1907 Edward VII arrived by Royal Train at Hixon station and was driven to Ingestre Hall in one of Lord Shrewsbury's fleet of cars. This was the beginning of a five-day visit. During that time the King visited Alton Towers, another of Lord Shrewsbury's houses, Rangemore Hall near Burton-on-Trent, and Stafford. On the Thursday of his visit he was shown Ingestre Park, famous for its deer, and walked in the Hall gardens. He also planted this cedar of Lebanon tree at the Mount, in the grounds, to commemorate his visit.

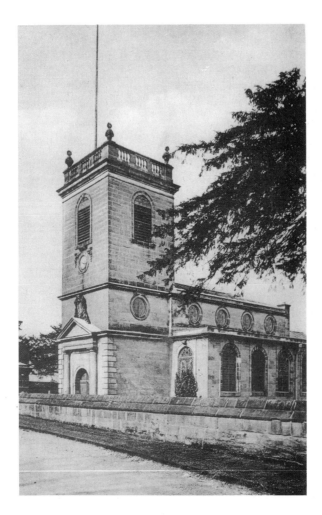

INGESTRE CHURCH

The old church at Ingestre, used as a private chapel by the Chetwynds, was pulled down and the present church built in its place in 1671. It has been claimed as one of the few examples of Sir Christopher Wren's work outside London. It is very unlikely that Wren worked here, but the style and quality of the building has suggested his influence. It has been called 'the finest Renaissance church outside London' and deserves to be better known. Notice how the outside is free from decoration except for the garlands round the clock and the shield over the pediment above the door.

INGESTRE CHURCH INTERIOR, 1907

The church interior retains nearly all its 1671 decor and furniture. The magnificent oak screen, carved with flowers, angels and cherubs and topped with the Royal Arms, can be seen clearly. The pulpit on the right is similarly carved. This was the first church in the county to be lit by electricity. In 1886 it was linked to the generators at Ingestre Hall. The six wrought iron fittings, each with two lamps which are still in use today, can be seen in the picture above.

MILFORD STATION, 1910

Milford and Brocton station, to give it its correct title, was not opened until thirty years after the Trent Valley railway line had been built. On bank holidays the platform was crowded with passengers brought by special excursion trains from Stafford and elsewhere. In the evening, long queues stretched from the station far down the road, as all those who had spent a day on the Chase waited to catch a train to take them home.

The station closed for passenger traffic in 1950, and for goods six years later.

STATION ROAD ON MILFORD DAY, MILFORD, 1906

A special excursion train from Stafford has unloaded its passengers at the station on the opposite page. They have climbed the steps from the platform to the road, crossed the bridge, which can be seen in the distance, and are streaming down to Milford Common past the boundary wall of the Shugborough estate on the right. Milford Day was an invention of the postcard publisher, but scenes like this were repeated every Easter, Whitsun and August bank holiday. Note the long skirts and large hats worn by women for a day on the Chase.

MILFORD, ON MILFORD DAY.

MILFORD, EASTER BANK HOLIDAY, 1906

Fosset's circus and fair first stopped at Milford in the 1880s. It proved a huge attraction and, by 1906, fairs were held on the Common every bank holiday in spring and summer. Some of the gypsy caravans and tents for various attractions can be seen in the distance. The three pictures on pages 63-65 were probably all taken on the same day.

THE DONKEYS ON MILFORD CHASE.

THE DONKEYS ON MILFORD CHASE, 1906

Another bank holiday view of Milford Chase, or Common. The donkeys were one of the great attractions
for children. It seems that most of the riders were boys — perhaps girls were hampered by their long skirts.
In the background, among other attractions, can be seen one end of the swingboats, and a coconut shy.
One of the boys on the right has already won himself a coconut.

THE BARLEY MOW, MILFORD, 1908

In the early-twentieth century Milford was a popular venue for cyclists, pedestrians who found the walk from Stafford or Rugeley not too energetic, and those who drove out in carriages. The focus was the Barley Mow, an old inn that had been enlarged and renovated in the 1880s. By 1909 it advertised 'a bowling green, quoiting and tennis grounds'. Since then the ground floor has been much altered with a new entrance and an extension, but the Barley Mow of today is easily recognisable in this 1908 view.

CLUB OUTING TO MILFORD, 1921

In the 1920s the spread of motor buses and charabancs added to the crowds at Milford. At Easter 1927 *The Staffordshire Advertiser* reported that on Sunday 8,000 people had been conveyed to Milford by bus, and that on Monday this had risen to 10,000 'The bus companies' resources have been severely taxed', commented the reporter. The Barley Mow was a popular venue for club outings. This unknown Stafford men's club was photographed there in August 1921. Note the variety of hats — bowlers, trilbys, flat caps, and straw boaters.

Courtship, Milford, Brocton Camp.

MILFORD COMMON, 1916

If you climb up the low hill at Milford until you reach as group of oak trees, you can look back, as this photographer did in 1916. He saw the Barley Mow to the left, the Red House with its long fence in the centre, and the railway signal box in the distance. Today the view is much the same, with Boston's garage and some new houses added. When the postcard was published in 1916 it was titled, 'Courtship, Milford' and a soldier from Brocton Camp, with his girl, was posed in the foreground. After the war the postcard was retitled 'The Green, Milford'.

THE ROCK HOUSE, MILFORD, 1927

The popularity of Milford led to a demand for tea-rooms and boarding apartments. One of several such establishments was The Rock House Boarding Apartments, opened by George De Vall in 1912. In 1927 this was taken over as tea-rooms by E. J. Garside, for whom this postcard was published. The next owners were the Bostons, who added a petrol filling station in front of the tea-rooms. Teas were served by waitresses in the front room of the house, while the long shed on the right was for self-service customers. In 1963 the house was pulled down and replaced by a garage.

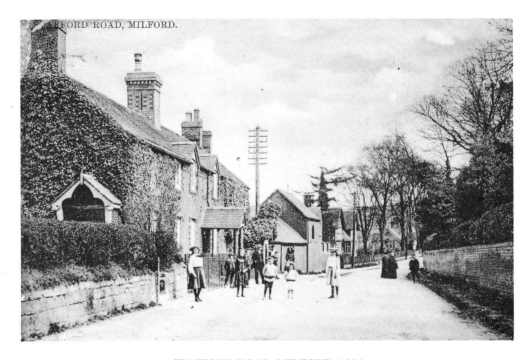

STAFFORD ROAD, MILFORD, 1906

This view of Stafford Road looking east has hardly changed since the postcard was published in 1906. The house on the left is still there, although the hedge has gone, and the wall is now only a foot high. In the distance are the outbuildings of the Home Farm (now a farm shop) and the Home Farm itself.

STAFFORD ROAD, MILFORD.

STAFFORD ROAD, MILFORD, 1906

The White House on the left has the date 1797 on one of its rainwater pipes and is rumoured to have been a beerhouse for canal bargees at one time. After this postcard was published, the house was extended when the White House Stores were added. Coincidentally, the owners were named White. Later the village post office and telephone exchange were also here. Notice the ladies' cycling dress of the period, and the absence of traffic which allowed them to pose safely in the road for the photographer.

SISTER DORA CONVALESCENT HOSPITAL, MILFORD, 1905

Sister Dora, or Dorothy Pattison, was famous for her work in nursing the poor at Walsall. After her death, £2,000 was raised by public subscription to build this hospital as a memorial to her. Its 16 beds allowed convalescent patients, some of whom can be seen on this postcard, to recuperate in the pure, bracing air of the Chase for a small weekly payment — or free if you had a ticket from one of the subscribers. Today, enlarged by a new block added behind the old building, 'Sister Dora' is a comfortable rest home for the elderly.

MILFORD CHASE, 1906

These hills and gullies overlooking Milford are still recognisable today. Notice the number of people scrambling up the hill, as well as the children and adults who willingly paused during their day out on the Chase to pose for the photographer. Note, too, the way children were dressed for a day out in 1906.

GOLF HOUSE, MILFORD, 1910

The Cannock Chase Golf Club was formed in 1894 and built the Golf House seen in the centre of this picture in 1898. The course was laid out over part of the Chase which was leased from Lord Lichfield at an annual rent of one shilling. In the foreground can be seen the green at the fourth hole the tee being away to the right. In 1920 the annual subscription was three guineas, and the green fee for visitors staying with members was two shillings and sixpence a day.

THE GOLF HOUSE, MILFORD, 1917

This is another drawing by Horace Overton Jones of the Ivy House, Colwich (see page 8). The Golf House was built of brick with cement facing and thatched with Norwegian rushes. In March 1922 a spark from the chimney set the rushes alight and, although much of the furniture and equipment was saved, shortage of water nearby prevented the fire being brought under control before the roof collapsed. It was not rebuilt.

Brocton Hall, Stafford.

BROCTON HALL, 1920

Brocton Hall, built in 1801, belonged to the Chetwynd family until 1922. In that year Mary Chetwynd sold the Hall and 120 acres of land to what is now the Brocton Hall Golf Club. The club had lost its clubhouse by fire earlier in the year and was having difficulties with its course, laid out over parts of the Chase where there was public access. A new 18-hole course was designed by Harry Vardon. The top floor of the Hall, occupied by the Club Secretary, was badly damaged by fire in 1939. After the fire the top floor was removed and the building re-roofed.

POOL LANE, BROCTON, 1907

As you travel from Milford towards Brocton, the left hand side of the road is open to the Chase until you reach the part of Pool Lane shown in this postcard, where houses begin on both sides of the road. Here the road was blocked by a gate to prevent animals straying from the Chase into the village. By 1907 the gate was almost off its hinges and probably disused. To the right is a smaller gate for those on foot. Today the house on the right still stands, and on the grass verge is a stone stump, the remains of a gatepost. The house on the left was pulled down to allow road widening.

THE GREEN, BROCTON, 1914

This postcard shows The Green, looking east, with Pool Lane to the right and Chase Road off picture to the left. In the centre is Green Farm, with Brocton Mission hall to the right of it. Brother Booth, a lay evangelist, began services in Brocton in 1889 and collected money to build the Hall, which opened in 1891. In 1951 the Hall was fully dedicated as All Saints Church and has since been added to and extended.

THE GREEN, BROCTON, 1915

This postcard shows The Green, looking west from near the junction of Sawpit Lane and Walton Lane. On the far side of The Green was the smithy. This is just out of sight in this picture, but some of the carts awaiting repair can be seen. Chase Road climbs the hill in the background and the houses on it are still recognisable, although more obscured by trees today. The Mission hall is on the right.

OLDACRE LANE, 1914
Oldacre Lane, leading to Oldacre Hall and the Chase, was a rural lane in 1914, with no houses along its
length except these cottages, about half way along its east side.

The Chase, Brocton

THE CHASE, BROCTON, 1930

In the foreground Chase Road winds down to Brocton village. This is the line taken by the road to Brocton Camp, built in 1915. The older track can be seen to the right of the road, passing in front of the homestead, with its fields enclosed out of the Chase. Today the older track can still be seen passing in front of several modern houses. This part of the Chase is now covered with trees and is almost unrecognisable.

Brocton Village, Dickens Series No. 3

ROADWORKS FOR BROCTON CAMP, 1915

The rapid expansion of the army after the outbreak of war in 1914 demanded additional army camps. One of these was Brocton Camp, on the Chase above Brocton and on either side of Chase Road. The Camp was marked out in January 1915 and the first huts occupied the following summer. This postcard shows a team of council roadmen and Royal Engineers with a steam roller improving Chase Road in May or June 1915 so that it could take traffic to the camp.

Military Police, Brocton Village. 21

MILITARY POLICE IN BROCTON, 1915

When the Camp was first opened, security was strict. In June 1915 one workman wrote on a postcard showing birch trees on the Chase, 'This is where we work, only you can't see any huts. No photos allowed'. A cyclist who stopped on the Chase to write a postcard to his mother reported that he was moved on by a mounted army patrol. This postcard shows military police on duty at the foot of Chase Road in November 1915.

L AND M LINES, BROCTON CAMP, 1917

'Wooden buildings of a depressing uniformity arranged in irritating and parallel straight lines' was the
Staffordshire Advertiser's description of the Camp. In this view the photographer is looking north-east
across the Oldacre Valley to L and M Lines. The writer of the card tells his mum that his hut is the top hut
in L Lines. He had marked it with an arrow. There is no explanation for the second arrow on the right.

CHURCH PARADE, BROCTON CAMP, 1916

This postcard shows the 9th (Reserve) Battalion of the Lincolnshire Regiment on church parade outside the Church Army Hut at Brocton Camp. C.E.M.S. stands for Church of England Men's Society. The hut had a simple altar at one end and recreational space at the other. In the words of one soldier, 'This is where we get our coffee, cakes, fags and stamps'.

The Home Hut, J Lines, Brocton Camp 64

HOME HUT, J LINES, BROCTON CAMP, 1916

The Home Hut for 'other ranks' was run by volunteers. Notice the cast-iron heating stove with a hot water or tea urn on top, the wooden chairs and general sparseness of decoration, apart from the Union Jack. The sender of this postcard tells his sweetheart, 'We have a short service here every evening and I pop in whenever I can.' J Lines was to the west of Chase Road.

OFFICERS.CLUB BROCTON.

OFFICERS' CLUB, BROCTON CAMP, 1916

Contrast the furnishings of this hut with those of the Home Hut for 'other ranks' on the opposite page. Later in the war the hut was taken over as a recreation hut for 'other ranks' on courses at the School of Musketry established in T Lines. The private who sent this postcard while on a course in 1917 wrote, 'They have taken up the carpets and removed the fancy covers off the tables since we took over the hut.'

CAMP, BROCTON.

TO GREET YOU.

THERE are places in England to Brocton superior,
In fact, it was known long ago as Siberia!
My word! it is like it,—from towns far away,—
Nothing but Khaki to make the place gay.

It's not too exciting as you may well guess,
For shops there are few and trains there are less,
But men there are plenty to cross the blue sea,
A fine lot of fellows—of course counting me!

Each man has his fairy, not always a Mary,
He thinks of her much as he sings "Tipperary,"
He marches right briskly under weight of his pack,
And dreams that "C.B." only means "coming back"!

And this is from one of them to wish you "good luck,"
He is hoping to prove he's not wanting in pluck,
Here's a handful of love from lone Cannock Chase,
From a lad who just longs for a sight of your face!

[Copyright.]   C.F.P.

BROCTON CAMP, 1916
Postcards with verses were popular with the troops. Verses like the one on this card could be printed with the name of any camp in the second line and a suitable view added above it. On this card Sapper Woodman wrote to his girl, 'We are getting put through it very stiff, but there are comforts we shouldn't have in France.'

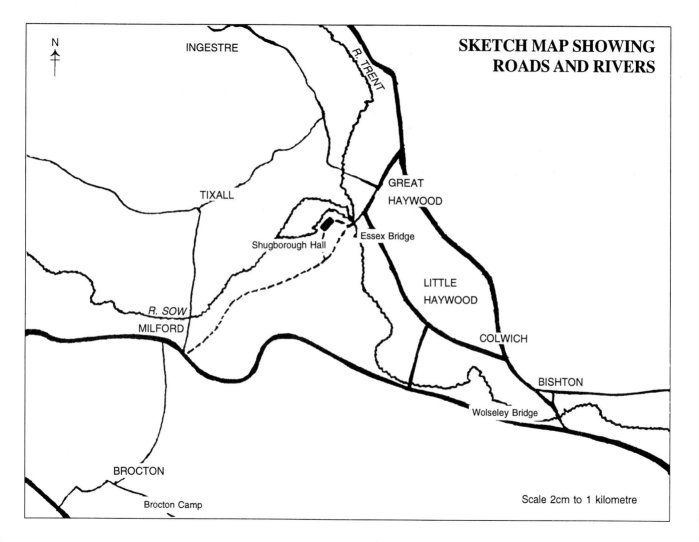

SKETCH MAP SHOWING
ROADS AND RIVERS

N

INGESTRE

R. TRENT

TIXALL

GREAT
HAYWOOD

Shugborough Hall

Essex Bridge

LITTLE
HAYWOOD

R. SOW

MILFORD

COLWICH

BISHTON

Wolseley Bridge

BROCTON

Brocton Camp

Scale 2cm to 1 kilometre

89

Other local titles published by S.B. Publications in the series 'A Portrait in Old Picture Postcards':

Bootle, Vols 1 & 2
Liverpool, Vols 1 & 2
Old Bebington
Rock Ferry, New Ferry and Bebington
Southport

Chester, Vols 1 & 2
Crewe, Vols 1 & 2
The Villages of West Cheshire
The Dane Valley

The Lost Villages of Manchester
The Manchester Ship Canal

Aston Villa
Bournville
Pershore and District
The Black Country, Vols 1 & 2
Walsall and District
Wolverhampton, Vols 1 & 2

Aberystwyth, Vols 1 & 2
Bangor
Chirk and the Glyn Valley Tramway
Connah's Quay & Shotton
Hawarden
Llandudno
Rhyl
Ruthin and District
Snowdonia

Shrewsbury
Wellington

Potteries Picture Postcards
Newcastle-under-Lyme
Stafford and District
Staffordshire Moorlands
Keele and Madeley
Stone and District
Mining Memories
Jarrow & Hebburn

Other local titles available and in preparation. For full details send SAE to: S.B. Publications, C/o 19 Grove Road, Seaford, East Sussex, BN25 1TP.